An Oak Tree Has a Life Cycle

by Debra Castor

Table of Contents

Words to Think About

life cycle

An oak tree changes and grows during its life cycle.

plants

Many types of plants live on Earth.

roots

Roots usually grow under the ground.

seeds

Most plants begin as seeds.

stems

Stems bring water and nutrients to plants.

trunk

A tree has a trunk.

Introduction

All **plants** have a **life cycle**, or an order in which they change and grow.

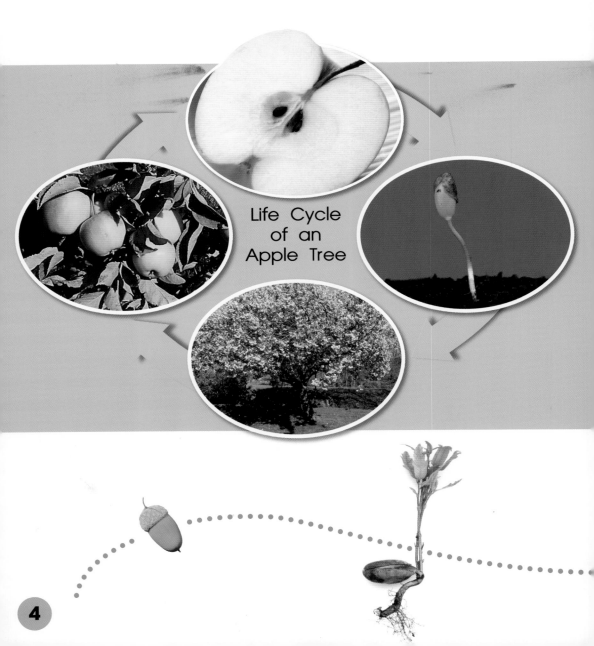

Life Cycle
of an
Apple Tree

During the life cycle, a plant grows the parts it needs to stay alive and to make new plants.

Life Cycle of a Tomato Plant

Oak trees have a life cycle. Fully grown oak trees can make new oak trees.

A New Oak Tree Begins

At first, a fully grown oak tree drops **seeds**. These seeds are acorns.

▲ This acorn fell from an oak tree.

▲ This squirrel found an acorn on the ground.

Animals will eat most of the acorns, but a few acorns will become new oak trees.

A New Oak Tree Grows

A few months after the acorn falls, **roots** begin to grow. The roots grow into the ground.

roots

▲ Roots grow if the acorn stays moist and cool.

Next, a **stem** grows from the acorn. Leaves grow from the stem during the first year. Now the oak tree is a sapling.

stem

leaves

Plant Fact

An oak tree is a seedling before it is a sapling.

Slowly, the oak tree becomes larger. At last, the stem becomes a thick, strong **trunk**.

trunk

stem

Flowers grow on the oak tree and then the flowers become acorns. What will happen to these acorns?

oak tree flower

acorns

LOOK AT TEXT STRUCTURE

Sequence of Events

This book shows a sequence, or order, of events. Find the words "at last." These words help you understand the sequence. What other words in this book help you understand the sequence?

11

Chapter 3

An Old Oak Tree Dies

After dropping acorns for many years, the oak tree finally dies. An oak tree can live for hundreds of years.

▲ Finally, the oak tree dies.

▲ This oak tree is about 1,500 years old.

Can you see oak trees where you live?

▲ This new oak tree grows in a forest.

Conclusion

An oak tree is a plant that changes and grows. An oak tree has a life cycle.

acorns

oak tree

roots

stem and leaves

Glossary

life cycle the order of how a living thing changes as it grows

See page 4.

plants living things that make their own food and stay in one place as they grow

See page 4.

roots parts of plants that are usually under the ground

See page 8.

seeds parts of plants that grow into new plants

See page 6.

stems parts of plants that carry water and nutrients

See page 9.

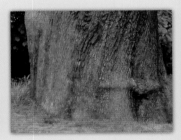

trunk the stem of a grown tree

See page 10.

Index